W9-BSK-744

50

Powerful Ideas You Can Use to Keep Your Customers

2nd Edition

By
Paul R. Timm, Ph.D.

50

Powerful Ideas You Can Use to Keep Your Customers

2nd Edition

By
Paul R. Timm, Ph.D.

CAREER PRESS
3 Tice Road
P.O. Box 687
Franklin Lakes, NJ 07417
1-800-CAREER-1
201-848-0310 (NJ and outside U.S.)
FAX: 201-848-1727

Copyright © 1995 by Paul R. Timm

All rights reserved under the Pan-American and International Copyright Conventions. This book may not be reproduced, in whole or in part, in any form or by any means electronic or mechanical, including photocopying, recording, or by any information storage and retrieval system now known or hereafter invented, without written permission from the publisher, The Career Press.

Note: Information given in this book is correct to the best of the authors' knowledge, but its accuracy is not guaranteed. Investment discussions are not meant to be advice, but a starting point for educated decisions.

50 POWERFUL IDEAS YOU CAN USE TO KEEP YOUR CUSTOMERS, 2ND EDITION
ISBN 1-56414-155-1, $7.99
Cover design by Digital Perspectives
Printed in the U.S.A. by Book-mart Press

To order this title by mail, please include price as noted above, $2.50 handling per order, and $1.00 for each book ordered. Send to: Career Press, Inc., 3 Tice Road, P.O. Box 687, Franklin Lakes, NJ 07417.

Or call toll-free 1-800-CAREER-1 (Canada: 201-848-0310) to order using VISA or MasterCard, or for further information on books from Career Press.

Library of Congress Cataloging-in-Publication Data

Timm, Paul R.
    50 powerful ideas you can use to keep your customers / by Paul R. Timm. -- 2nd ed.
        p. cm.
    Includes index.
    ISBN 1-56414-155-1 : $7.99
    1. Vocational guidance. 2. Self-presentation. 3. Job security.
I. Title. II. Title: Fifty powerful ideas you can use to keep your customers.
HF5381.T5664 1995
658.8'12--dc20

94-44541
CIP

Contents

Section I

Service: The Master Key to Career Success

Regardless of your job title, position in an organization or experience, *your number-one task* will always be to attract, satisfy and preserve customers. And *everyone has customers.*

This book is about the advantages that come to *you* when you give great customer service. The specific tips are easy to apply. And they'll get results.

But before we get into the *50 Powerful Ideas,* let's talk about who your customers are, what they can do for you and what happens if you "lose" one.

Who are your customers and what can they do for you?

Customers. For many of us, these are easy to identify. They buy things from us. But some people will say, "I don't work directly with customers." Before you accept this idea, I suggest a closer look at just who exactly our customers are. Everybody has customers.

In organizations, customers take two forms, *internal* and *external.*

Internal and external customers

Internal customers are those people, departments or organizations served by what we do. The only person who might have no internal customers is the individual who works completely alone. For the rest of us, internal customers are a fact of life.

For example, a word-processing clerk or copy center worker within a company serves other workers' needs for documents-handling for the larger organization. A personnel office worker serves employees' needs for benefits information, management's needs for staffing, and company legal people's needs for handling various government paperwork requirements.

Everyone has at least one internal customer: his boss; managers also have internal customers in the form of the people they supervise. They rely on us to meet their needs.

External customers are those people or departments who are the end users of our organization's products or services. This is, of course, the traditional use of the term "customer:"

Often we call these people different names depending on our business: We call them customers, clients, guests, patients, patrons, cases, franchisees, passengers, students and the like.

To keep things simple, this book will use the generic term "customer" throughout. But please bear in mind that you probably serve a number of different types of customers and you may call them something different.

Satisfied customers are those who purchase (although not always for money) and receive value from the goods and services you offer. Generally these customers have a choice. If they don't like what you offer or the way you offer it, they can go elsewhere for similar goods or services. When they do, you and your organization suffer. Satisfied customers create profits. Profits, in turn create organizational success and the ability to pay employees.

Some organizations however have "captive customers." They provide a service customers can't get elsewhere. Public utilities and government agencies are examples. Customers can't shop around for electric power or license plates. This brings up the question:

Why give good service if the customer has no choice but to deal with you?

It's easy to see how keeping customers happy is important to the health of for-profit organizations, but why be so concerned with service in nonprofit, monopolistic or government agencies? After all, where else will they buy what we sell? Here's why:

In the government agency, public utility or nonprofit organization, customer displeasure with service quickly becomes customer animosity. This animosity can snowball. As customers come to expect that they're going to be treated poorly, they in fact will begin to treat employees poorly (in "self-defense"). The attacked employee fights back and the stress on both parties mounts.

Some results of this stress on employees and the organization:

- Increased stress-related illness.
- Employee burnout and absenteeism.
- Higher turnover—people quit.
- Cost and inconvenience of training replacement employees.
- Increased difficulty in attracting good employees to the job.
- Negative public view of the organization.
- Lower sense of pride in the organization.
- Lower sense of self-worth among employees.
- Increased defensiveness in employees, which can lead to even more stress.

Very few people can put up with the day-to-day barrage of unhappy patrons who expect to be treated poorly.

The best reason to give good service is that it makes you feel better.

At the most basic level we are all motivated to act in a particular way because our action will either:

- Result in a gain (reward)

  or

- Avoid a loss (punishment)

Giving good customer service, even in nonprofit situations, can satisfy both motivations for the giver. People who provide good customer service—regardless of the nature of their business—earn psychological benefits in addition to any rewards offered by their organizations.

If you are frustrated or unhappy in your job now, take an objective look at the kind of service you are giving. In almost every case, your job satisfaction mirrors the satisfaction people feel when doing business with you. Giving poor service is a way of beating up on yourself!

So regardless of the profit aims of your organization, giving good service makes sense for you as an individual. It also makes a lot of sense for you as a member of an organization. Organizational success often affects your individual success. So let's talk about service and your organization.

Good news and bad news

When it comes to organizational success with customers, I have good news and bad news. First the bad news: The average American company will lose 10 to 30 percent of its customers this year—mostly because of poor service. When customers have a choice, they'll go to the competition almost one-third of the time.

Customer satisfaction is like an election held every day, and the people vote with their feet. If dissatisfied, they walk (sometimes run) to your competitor.

When your customers don't have a choice—such as in dealing with public utilities or government agencies—they'll use their feet for something else: they'll kick you. Customer dissatisfaction will erupt in the form of animosity directed toward you and your organization. Public relations efforts alone will provide little more than a bandage. The psychological toll on employees will result in higher turnover and additional costs as these burned-out workers need to be retrained or replaced.

Now the good news. Organizations that initiate effective customer retention programs have seen profits jump 25 to 100 percent. Nonprofit groups see reduced turnover, better financial results and happier staffs.

Like it or not, customer service is the competitive battleground for the 1990s and beyond. In fact, it will always be the decisive battleground.

Most people accept, or at least give lip service to the idea that "the customer is the boss." We talk about the customer "always being right." We say that the customer is "our reason for existing" as an organization. But the real management challenge lies in translating these slogans into actions that convey these feelings and beliefs to the customer.

Even when leaders truly believe in the importance of customer service, they still face the difficulty of getting the customer contact people to do what customers want. The problem gets trickier when we see that the lowest paid and least well-trained employees are often those who face the customer every day.

- A multi-million dollar fast-food operation, for example, places its success squarely in the hands of the minimum-wage teenager taking the orders and delivering the food.

- The image of a multi-billion dollar bank is created in the mind of the customer by the entry-level teller who handles his day-to-day transactions.

- A multi-billion dollar government agency is judged largely by the receptionist who answers the phone or greets the customer, thus setting a tone for any transaction. (Many a criticism of the "government bureaucracy" can be traced to the attitudes of a receptionist.) An otherwise pleasant transaction can be poisoned by "getting off on the wrong foot."

Customer service is the master key to success for each of us as individuals and for the organizations we work in. This book tells how to use that key. But first, let's look at the downside. What happens when we give poor service and the customer quits being a customer?

The terrible cost of the lost customer

Most people don't understand the real cost of a lost customer. When an unhappy customer decides to stop doing business with us, the costs are much more than we realize.

To get a clearer view of the real costs, let's consider a business we can all identify with: a grocery supermarket. Here's a story of Mrs. Williams, a lady who has been shopping at Happy Jack's Supermarket[1] for many years, but who has decided to stop shopping there. Although a regular customer for years, she has never felt that her business is appreciated.

As you read, try to calculate the cost of these same "ripple effects" on your company.

Good-bye Mrs. Williams

There goes Mrs. Williams. She just checked out her groceries from Happy Jack's Supermarket and she's mad as hell. She's been shopping there for years but the produce man wouldn't even consider making her a smaller package of apples, the dairy department was out of the quart-size skim milk and then the cashier demanded two forms of identification with her check. What do they think she is, a common criminal?

But worst of all was just an overall feeling that Happy Jack's employees do not care whether she shops there. She spends about 50 hard-earned dollars there every week, but to the store employees she's just another cash cow to be milked without so much as a sincere "thank-you." Nobody seems to care whether she's a satisfied customer.

But today is different. Mrs. Williams just decided to try shopping elsewhere. Maybe—just maybe—there is a store where they'll appreciate her business.

---

[1] All names are fictitious. If there is a "Happy Jack's Supermarket" somewhere, it's not the one described in this story.

What do the employees think about that?

They're not worried. Happy Jack's is a pretty big chain and doesn't really need Mrs. Williams. Besides, she can be a bit cranky at times. They'll survive without her $50 a week. Too bad she's unhappy, but a big company like this can't twist itself into contortions just to save one little old lady from going down the street to the competition.

Sure, we believe in treating customers well, but we're business people. Let's look at the bottom line. After all, it can hardly be considered a major financial disaster to lose a few customers like Mrs. Williams. Or can it?

The employees at Happy Jack's need to understand some economic facts of life. Successful businesses look long term. They look at the "ripple effects" of their service, not just at the immediate profit from an individual purchase.

The shortsighted employee sees Mrs. Williams as a small customer dealing with a big company. Let's look at the situation from another, longer-term perspective.

More than the loss of one small customer

The loss of Mrs. Williams is not, of course, a $50 loss. It's much, much more. She was a $50-a-week buyer. That's $2,600 a year or $26,000 over a decade. Perhaps she would shop at Happy Jack's for a lifetime, but we'll use the more conservative 10-year figure for illustration.

But ripple effects make it much worse. Studies show that *an upset customer tells, on average, 11 other people about an unhappy experience.* Some people will tell many more, but let's assume that Mrs. Williams told 11. The same studies say that these 11 *may tell an average of five others each.* This could be getting serious!

How many people are likely to hear the bad news about Happy Jack's? Look at the math:

Mrs. Williams	1
tells 11 others	+11
who each tell five	+55
Total who heard	**67**

Sure, but all 67 of these people aren't going to rebel against Happy Jack's, are they? Probably not. Let's assume that of these 67 customers or potential customers, only 25 percent decide not to shop at Happy Jack's. Twenty-five percent of 67 (rounded) is 17.

Assuming that these 17 people would also be $50-a-week shoppers, Happy Jack's stands to lose $44,200 a year, or $442,000 in a decade because Mrs. Williams was upset when she left the store.

Although these numbers are starting to get alarming, they are still conservative. A typical supermarket customer actually spends about $100 a week, so losing a different customer could quickly double these figures.

Take a moment to think about how much money your customer spends with you. Perhaps he or she buys every month or two or only once every few years. But in almost every case, repeat business is crucial to your success. Viewing customers as one-time buyers can and will be hazardous to your financial health.

How much will it cost to replace these customers?

Customer service research says that *it costs about six times as much to attract a new customer* (mostly advertising and promotion costs) *than it does to keep an existing one* (where costs may include giving refunds, offering samples, replacing merchandise). One report put these figures at about $19 to keep a customer happy versus $118 to get a new buyer into the store.

Some quick math shows the real cost of the lost Mrs. Williams:

- Cost of keeping Mrs. Williams happy—$19
- Cost of attracting 17 new customers—$2,006

How lost customers can mean lost jobs

The Robert Half Organization, a well-known personnel consulting firm, shows a simple way to calculate the amount of sales needed to pay employees' salaries. Assuming that a company pays 50 percent in taxes and earns a profit of 5 percent after taxes, the following chart shows how much must be sold to pay each employee (in three different salary levels) and maintain current profit levels:

Salary	Benefits	After tax cost	Sales needed
$25,000	$11,500	$18,250	$365,000
$15,000	$6,900	$10,950	$219,000
$10,000	$4,600	$7,300	$146,000

These figures will vary, of course. But the impact on one's job can be clearly shown.

If a $10,000-a-year clerk irritates as few as three or four customers *in a year*, the ripple effects can exceed the amount of sales needed to maintain that job! Unfortunately, many organizations have employees who irritate three or four customers *a day!* Ouch.

Applying Mrs. Williams to your company

What do Mrs. Williams and the grocery store example have to do with you and your business? Basically, the same things can happen. Your unhappy customer will tell other customers or potential customers. They in turn will tell even more people.

Let's take a few moments to go back to the Mrs. Williams example, but instead use your own organization. Suppose you lose one customer and some of the other statistics hold true. Take a few moments to calculate on the next page the numbers as they apply to your organization.

If you work for a nonprofit or government agency where the dollar sales are not a relevant measure, calculate on the next page the number of people who may be aggravated or upset with you and your organization. Think in terms of the psychological price that must be paid as you deal with frustrated, angry, upset patrons on a day-to-day basis.

The front-line team makes all the difference

The customer game is ultimately won or lost on the front lines—where the customer comes in contact with employees. The front line team *is* the company in the customer's eyes. Therefore the front line team must see themselves as the heroes they genuinely are. Managers must support them with the tools (training, systems)

Calculating the cost of your lost customer

Average or typical dollar amount spent
    per person: $_____
Annual dollar amount: $_____
Decade dollar amount: $_____

Annual dollar amount x 17 (people who may
    follow an unhappy customer out the door): $_____

Annual revenue lost: $_____

Then,
Add customer replacement costs of
    17 customers x ($118 is a
    typical figure): $_____

Minus the cost of keeping your present
    customer happy ($19 is a typical figure) $_____
    (E.g., $19 x # of present customers)

"Replacement" costs: $_____

Finally,
Total the revenue lost figures (annual or per decade)
    plus replacement costs

A rough cost of your loss: $_____

Note: These calculations are designed only to get you thinking about the ripple effects of unhappy customers. Their mathematical precision is not guaranteed nor is it very important. The point is, lost customers cost a lot of money.

needed to serve the customer heroically. Surprisingly, all too few firms understand this.[2]

Saving a fraction of the "cost of the lost" can solidify a company's competitive position. Profits maintained can be spent improving employee work environment, giving raises or keeping good people employed.

The magic of *E-Plus* thinking

Much of this book builds around one central theme. It's simple to state, but implementation takes some creativity. In the bonus chapter at the end of the book I will show you a step-by-step approach to implementing this theme in the form of an operational strategy—a way of doing business that will pay enormous dividends. But first, a description of the underlying premise, the central theme:

> *We can achieve exceptional customer satisfaction and retention by exceeding customer expectations in positive ways.*

The answers to every customer problem are not simple, but my research and consulting does point to a blueprint that can be used by any organization—and to what appears to be the "master key" I call *E-Plus*. First, some background...

---

[2] Tom Peters, *Thriving on Chaos*, Harper & Row Publishers, p. 213.

Why customers do what they do

At the most basic level, people are motivated to act in particular ways because their actions will either result in a gain (reward) or avoid a loss (punishment). Customers are rational people. If a buying experience is positive, they will probably come back; if negative, they'll try to avoid returning.

This is true to a point, but such motivation is not quite so clear cut. Management theorist Frederick Herzberg taught that the opposite of an unhappy worker (or customer) is not necessarily a motivated one. He taught that satisfaction and motivation are two separate factors, not two ends of the same scale. His theory caused us to rethink the relationship between satisfaction and motivation.

Applying this thinking to customer behaviors would suggest that customers who are satisfied may be *inert*, not motivated as earlier thinkers assumed. Their satisfaction is simply the *absence of dissatisfaction*, not the motivation to become a repeat customer. A "zone of indifference" lies between the dissatisfied and the motivated.

Dissatisfied   Satisfied   Motivated
↳ **(zone of indifference)** ↱

Herzberg would say that the satisfied person on the above model is one whose "hygiene" needs are met. He is not suffering dissatisfaction but is rather in a neutral state. His lower-level needs are met; the services he received were adequate. But for *motivation to return* to occur, something more than adequate satisfaction must be experienced.

The challenge, then, is to get beyond satisfaction to motivation. To do so, we must consider...

The crucial role of customer expectations

As a customer entering into a transaction, you expect (albeit perhaps unconsciously) to be treated a particular way. What we expect is often based on our past associations with this person or organization or ones we see as similar. (This similarity is highly subjective and may be unfounded if put to the test of rationality, but for us, it's real.) If we have had good experiences with that person or organization before, we'd probably expect something satisfactory. If the last transaction wasn't so positive, we might assume the next one wouldn't be better.

The part of all this that frustrates customer service people is that expectations are *perceptual*. They exist in the mind of our customer. Sometimes they are accurate and rational, sometimes they aren't. They present a moving, vaporous target.

When we judge the quality of a tangible product, we use more objective standards. For example, when we buy a new automobile, how do we judge its quality? We probably look at things like:

- Its reliability (its starts and runs well).
- Low frequency of repair (it seldom has to be fixed).
- Appropriate size (it holds my family comfortably).
- A good price relative to its quality (it looks nice but doesn't cost an arm and a leg).
- Workmanship (it seems to be well-built, it has a nice paint job).

Likewise when we judge the quality of a service (a house painter's job, for example) we measure it against such standards as:

- The work was done on time (he met the deadline).
- The surfaces to be painted were carefully prepared.
- The paints were mixed and applied neatly.
- The painter cleaned up after the job.

These kinds of standards are pretty predictable. They are much the same for each customer.

But evaluating the degree of customer satisfaction goes beyond the core product or service bought. The standards by which customers measure satisfaction are more ambiguous.

To further complicate matters, expectations will be different among organizations or under differing circumstances. When purchasing a tangible product, people expect different treatment from a "high-touch," full-service retailer than they do from a warehouse store. They expect different service from a prestigious law firm than a state auto license bureau.

For that matter, they probably expect something different from the same store at different times. Perhaps a little less personal attention is anticipated during busy periods (like Christmas shopping or end-of-month license plate buying).

Different expectations from different businesses

Suppose you intend to shop at a low cost, self-service discount store like a Kmart[3]. Going into the Kmart store, you expect to be treated in a particular way. You do not necessarily expect that the clerk in the clothing department (if you can find one) will be an expert in fitting clothing. Nor would you be likely to expect that person to be particularly helpful in choosing or color-coordinating items you may want to purchase. This is not to say that some people who work there do not have these skills, but we probably wouldn't expect them as a general rule.

If we simply select some clothing items from a rack and take them to a checkout for purchase, we are not surprised nor particularly disappointed. That's about what we expected, and if other aspects of the store are okay (it seems clean and well-stocked, for instance), we could be perfectly satisfied.

By contrast, if we were to go to a Nordstrom or Bloomingdale's full-service department store, we would expect a different kind of transaction. We would probably expect that a person working in a clothing department would have considerable expertise in clothing fit, color and materials. We might realistically expect that service person to give us some attention and assistance as we make our purchases.

When we find situations like these just described, our expectations are met. Dissatisfaction is probably avoided; we are in that zone of indifference.

---

[3] I use Kmart only as an example because of its familiarity to readers. No critical evaluation of Kmart or any other organizations named in this book is intended.

The key to exceptional customer satisfaction and motivation to return, however, lies not in meeting expectations but in *exceeding* them. More on that later.

One of three situations may arise as we compare our expectations with the service received:

Positive expectations failed		Negative expectations failed
	Expectations met	
Negative expectations confirmed		Positive or neutral expectations exceeded

In the condition described in the left column, the customer's experience was worse than expected. She's dissatisfied and likely to defect to another provider, if she has a rational alternative. The middle column customer is neither dissatisfied nor particularly motivated to return. This is the zone of indifference I spoke of earlier.

In the right column situation, the transaction was better than expected. Either the customer thought it would be pretty good and it was very good, or the customer thought it wouldn't be so good but it wasn't as bad as expected. If positive expectations were sufficiently exceeded (or negative ones shown to be unfounded), this customer is a very good candidate for repeat business.

The right column situation is what I call an *E-Plus* experience—customer expectations were *exceeded*.

Why *E-Plus* leads to customer retention

Next, let me show you some theoretical basis for predicting that the *E-Plus* (right column) customer will become a repeat customer.

Why can we predict that the customer whose expectations are exceeded will return? A theory founded in social psychology called *Equity Theory* gives a rationale.

Psychologist J. Stacy Adams first articulated this theory in the mid 1960s. It has stood the test of time to be widely accepted as a predictor of some kinds of human behavior. Here is a quick summary of the theory:

Equity theory starts with the premise that people are constantly finding themselves in various kinds of relationships ranging from the intimate to the cursory. The buyer-seller relationship is germane to this discussion.

Once in a relationship, we constantly assess the relative equity of our involvement compared to other people. We regularly check to see if what we give to the relationship balances with what we are getting out of it. We also compare our relative contribution to those of others.

Initially, much testing of this theory focused on the workplace where workers' perceptions of fairness (equity) were correlated with certain behaviors. Not surprisingly, studies found that people who were paid less for doing the same work as others, for example, felt a sense of inequity.

In my own doctoral dissertation, I found that employees who sensed that their supervisor communicated more often and more positively with other employees in the workgroup felt a clear sense of inequity.

But the theory goes beyond simply citing situations where people may feel inequitably treated. It also predicts what people would do about it.

When inequity is sensed, people will respond with one or some combination of the following:

- *Ignore or rationalize the inequity.* ("He deserves to be treated better than I," or "The world isn't fair but I'm not going to fight it.")

- *Demand restitution.* (The offended person goes to the boss to demand fairer pay or the customer wants his money back when product quality is poor.)
- *Retaliate.* (This can range from badmouthing the organization or person seen as the cause of the inequity to outright sabotage.)
- *Withdraw from the relationship.*

So far this theory seems to bear out common sense. If we feel we are being unfairly treated, we get upset and usually do something about it.

Hence, the unsatisfied participant in a relationship (the customer) is likely to do one of these things. The first two alternatives may give your business a chance to patch things up and retain the customer, but the last two can be devastating. Retaliation often takes the form of telling other people about poor service received. The average person tells 10 to 20 others, studies say. These negative ripple effects can result in scores or even hundreds of lost customers or potential customers.

But there is another side to equity theory that predicts this: People who feel they are receiving *more than they deserve* from a transaction also experience a psychological need to restore balance. A simple example is the social pressure you may feel to reciprocate when someone invites you to his or her home for dinner. The relationship will remain unbalanced until you rebalance it with a similar kindness.

Herein lies the theoretical basis for exceeding customer expectations. By going beyond the expected, you create an imbalance that, for many people, will require action on their part to rebalance. The logical options are the opposite of what the victim of a negative imbalance feels: he or she could rationalize or ignore it, of course. But attempts to restore the balance could also take the form of telling others of the positive experience, paying a premium for the goods received or becoming a repeat customer.

The challenge, then, is to *create positive imbalances by exceeding customer expectations.* This is the master key I call *E-Plus.* Using this master key requires two steps: Understanding customer expectations and exceeding them.

Therein lies the power of *E-Plus.* This book shows you at least 50 ways to exceed customer expectations.

The service revolution is now

Clearly a service revolution is taking place right now. We are free to choose our roles in this revolution. We can continue to grapple in the dark and assume that an occasional upset customer is of no major consequence to us. Or we can accept the fact that every customer is exceptionally valuable to our organization—and to our career success.

Now let's get on with those *50 Powerful Ideas You Can Use to Keep Your Customers.*

Section II

Powerful Ideas Anyone Can Use

To get off to a good start

1. Greet them like guests

Woody Allen once said that 80 percent of success is just showing up. In customer service, 80 percent of success is just treating the customer like a guest who just showed up.

When guests come to your home, you greet them, right? You say "hello," or "hi there." Yet we've all had the experience of being totally ignored by service people in some businesses. A friendly greeting is one of those little things that mean a lot.

Greet your customer promptly

A study clocked the number of seconds people had to wait to be greeted in several businesses. Researchers then asked customers how long they'd been waiting. In every case, the customer's estimate of the time elapsed was much longer than the actual time. A customer waiting 30 or 40 seconds often feels like she's been waiting three or four minutes! Time drags when you're waiting to be noticed.

A prompt greeting reduces customer stress. Why would a customer feel stress? Remember, she is probably on unfamiliar turf. She is likely to feel somewhat uncomfortable. You work there every day, she is just visiting.

A quick, friendly greeting starts to relax the customer and greases the wheels of smooth service.

Speak up. Verbally greet a customer within 10 seconds of the time she comes into your store or approaches your work location. Even if you are busy with another customer or on the phone, pause to say hello and let her know that you'll be ready to help her soon.

2. Talk to customers with your eyes

Even in situations where you may not be able to say hello out loud, you can make eye contact. Simply looking at your customer tells her much about your willingness to serve.

As with your greeting, the timing is important. The 10-second rule also applies here. Make eye contact with a customer within 10 seconds, even if you are busy with another person.

Eye contact creates a bond between you and the customer. It conveys your interest in communicating further.

Unlike the spoken greeting, you don't have to interrupt what you are doing with another customer. Just a pause and a quick look captures a new customer into an obligation to deal with you further, greatly reducing the chance she'll feel ignored and leave.

When working with customers, be sensitive to *how* you look at them. Communication expert Bert Decker says that the three "I's" of eye communication are intimacy, intimidation and involvement. Intimacy (like when we're expressing love) and intimidation (when we want to exert power) are both communicated by looking at another person for a long period—from 10 seconds to a minute or more.

But most communication in business settings calls for Decker's third "I"—involvement. In our culture, people create involvement by looking at the other person for five- to 10-second periods before looking away briefly. This is generally comfortable for people. If you look away more often than that, you may be seen as "shifty" or suspicious; if you lock in eye contact for longer, it may be seen as a suggestion of intimidation or intimacy.

I remember going into a very small watch repair shop. The proprietor was a real expert at repairing timepieces and his prices were good. But as I squeezed into his tiny shop he was serving another customer. I stood not more than five feet away from him for about five minutes before he acknowledged me. It got pretty uncomfortable. Once he finished with the customer ahead of me he was attentive and effective, but he ran a real risk of losing me before he got a chance to show me what he could do—simply because it was uncomfortable standing there without being acknowledged. All he would have needed to do was say hello and let me know that he would be with me momentarily.

3. Smile

As the old adage goes, "Smile. It'll make people wonder what you've been up to." But more importantly, it'll tell customers that they came to the right place and are on friendly ground.

Keep in mind that a smile originates in two places, the mouth and the eyes. A lips-only version looks pasted on, insincere. It's like saying "cheese" when being photographed. It doesn't fool anyone.

The eyes, however, are the windows to the soul and tell the truth about your feelings toward people.

So smile with your eyes and your mouth. Let your face show that you're glad your guest has arrived. Remember, you are not dressed for work until you put on a smile.

Now, in fairness, some people smile more readily than others. For some, a more serious facial expression is comfortable and natural. But in American culture, a smile is both expected and appreciated when one is meeting people. If you don't smile spontaneously, practice it. It need not be a Cheshire Cat, ear-to-ear grin (in fact that may *really* get people wondering about you), but just a pleasant, natural smile. Look, too, at your eyebrows. Some people knit their brows and appear to be scowling, even when they don't intend to. Look at yourself in the mirror. Work on facial expression as an actor might.

4. Break the ice

The best way to start a conversation depends on what the customer needs. In many cases, especially in retail stores, customers need first to be reassured that this is a "nice friendly place" to do business. They need to dispel worries about being high-pressured into buying something they don't want. Use a nonthreatening ice breaker.

Often customers want to browse; get the feel of the place before they commit to doing business.

The best ice breaker for the browser can be an off-topic, friendly comment. Some good ones might be:

- *A compliment.* ("That's a very sharp tie you're wearing," or "Your children are sure cute. How old are they?")
- *Weather-related.* ("Isn't this sunshine just beautiful?" or "Some snowfall, isn't it?")
- *Small talk.* (Look for cues about interests in sports, jobs, mutual acquaintances, past experiences, etc.)

If your browser seems to be focusing attention on a product (say she is holding several shirts or is looking at a particular line of products), she can be reclassified as a "focused shopper."

The best ice breaker for the focused shopper is one that is more specific to the buying decision. It may:

- *Anticipate the customer's questions.* ("What size are you looking for?" or "Can I help you select a ____?")
- *Provide additional information.* ("Those shirts are all 25 percent off today," or "We have additional sizes in the stock room.")
- *Offer a suggestion or recommendation.* ("Those stripe suits are really popular this season," or "If you need help with measurements our estimators can figure out what you'll need.")

Be attentive to the customers' needs. Give them time to browse if that's what they need, but be responsive to them in helping make a buying decision when they are ready to buy.

5. Get the customer doing something

Telling people about your products or services isn't usually enough. Showing them how it works is much better. But to really serve your customers, get them involved—get their hands on your products in some way and they'll feel better about you and your company.

Studies of successful computer saleopcople, for example, show that they encourage customers to sit down at the computer as soon as possible to get them playing with it. They don't dazzle (or confuse) the customer with hi-tech jargon or even information about the machine's capabilities. They get them *doing something*. Likewise, the best auto sales people invite customers to sit in and test drive the car right away.

Other ways to get people doing something:

- Personally hand them shopping carts or baskets.
- Ask them to begin filling out paperwork.
- Get them to touch the product.
- Offer a piece of candy or a fruit while they wait.
- Offer a product flier, information packet, video presentation or sample to review It doesn't matter so much *what* they do, so long as they begin to do *something*.

6. Watch your personal appearance and grooming

From the moment we meet people, we begin to size them up. We begin to draw conclusions about them almost immediately. What we decide about their trustworthiness and ability is largely a factor of first impressions. As the old saying goes, you only get one chance to make that first impression.

The key word in dress and grooming is *appropriate*. If in doubt about what is appropriate dress and grooming, look at what other successful people are doing. You need not be a copycat or wear an outfit you hate, but do consider what other role models do. And then meet or exceed their appearance.

An owner of an auto repair shop tried an experiment. Each of his repair people was paid on commission for the amount of repair work they did. He invited the mechanics to volunteer to change their dress and grooming. Several agreed to cut their hair shorter, shave daily and wear clean uniforms.

The outcome: Those who did created far more repeat business than the others. The customers would ask for the better dressed mechanics, and those who chose to dress and groom themselves in the "old way" found themselves getting less work.

But remember to dress appropriately. Salespeople in a surf shop would look foolish in three-piece suits; undertakers would look ludicrous in Hawaiian sport shirts. To overcome problems of individual differences that may be ineffective, some organizations issue uniforms. These may be coveralls, full uniforms or partial uniforms such as blazers, vests, name badges or workshirts. Some employees like these (they save on the costs of a wardrobe) while some resist the sameness of the uniformed look.

Determine what level of professionalism you want to convey to your customers, then create a look that projects your competence. Your customers notice these things.

7. Check the appearance of your work area

"A cluttered desk is the sign of a cluttered mind," says the desk plaque. A cluttered work area conveys a sense of disorganization and low professionalism.

Look around you and see what your customer sees. Is merchandise displayed attractively? Is the place clean and tidy? Does the workspace look like an organized, efficient place?

Check, too, for barriers. Often people arrange their workspace with a desk, counter or table between them and the customer. While sometimes this is necessary, often it creates a barrier—both physical and psychological—between the customer and the server. Try inviting customers to sit beside your desk with you instead of across from you.

Try using a small round table, especially when customers need to read materials you give them. Some auto dealerships have removed all sales office desks and replaced them with small round tables. Now the customer and sales person sit around the table and work together to make a deal. You don't feel like you are on opposite sides, in "combat" with each other, when the table is round.

Finally, look for customer comfort. Are your customers invited to sit in comfortable chairs? Does your office or store invite them to relax? Are waiting areas furnished with reading materials, perhaps TVs? Are vending machines available? Are the vending areas kept clean?

A small auto body shop I visited surprised me. It had a waiting room that looked like a living room in a nice home. Easy chairs, a TV, coffee table with recent magazines, even fresh flowers.

Recently, automakers have begun to emphasize ways to make their car lots and showrooms, many of which are decades old, more attractive and customer-friendly. Some now feature landscaped settings with benches and pathways, different display areas for each auto brand and interactive systems with screens that show how elements like paint colors and upholstery look together. Take a look at your work areas from the customer's viewpoint.[4]

8. Use good telephone techniques

Often your only contact with customers is via the telephone. Make the most of it.

A key to successful phone use is to simply *remember that your customer cannot see you.* Your challenge is to make up for all that lost nonverbal communication by using your voice effectively.

The best ways to use the phone effectively:

- *Give the caller your name.* Let the caller know who you are just as you would in a face-to-face situation (via a name tag or desk plaque).

- *Smile into the phone.* Somehow people can hear a smile over the phone! Some telephone pros place a mirror in front of them while they're on the phone.

---

[4] "A Picnic in a Car Lot?" in *Wall Street Journal*, October 13, 1994, p. A-1.

- *Keep your caller informed.* If you need to look up information, tell the customer what you are doing. Don't leave her holding a dead phone having no clue as to whether you are still with her.
- *Invite the caller to get to the point.* Use questions such as "How can I assist you today?" or "What can I do for you?"
- *Commit to requests of the caller.* Tell the caller specifically what you will do and when you will get back to her. ("I'll check on this billing problem and get back to you by five this afternoon, okay?")
- *Thank the caller.* This lets the caller know when the conversation is over.
- *Let your voice fluctuate in tone, rate and loudness.* You hold people's attention by putting a little life into your voice. Express honest reactions in expressive ways. Let your voice tones be natural and friendly.
- *Use hold carefully.* People hate being put on hold. When it's necessary, explain why and break in periodically to let them know they haven't been forgotten. If what you're doing will take longer than a few minutes, ask the caller if you can call her back. *Write down your commitment to call back and don't miss it.*
- *Use friendly, tactful words.* Never accuse the customer of anything; never convey that her request is an imposition.

An excellent 30-minute videotape training program featuring the author is *Winning Telephone Techniques* produced by JWA Video in Chicago. For information, call 312-829-5100. (See coupon on page 123.)

9. Say please and thank you

At the risk of sounding like one of those books about "things I learned in kindergarten," *be polite*. It may seem old-fashioned and some customers won't be as polite to you, but that's not *their* job.

In a recent "Dear Abby" column the writer complained about salespeople who say "there you go" to conclude a transaction. That kind of comment is not an appropriate substitute for thanking the customer.

"Please" and "thank you" are powerful words for building customer rapport and creating customer loyalty. They are easy to say and well worth the effort.

10. Enjoy people and their diversity

J.D. Salinger said, "I am a kind of paranoid in reverse. I suspect people of plotting to make me happy." With an attitude like that we'd look forward to every meeting with every customer.

Of course, we quickly learn that some customers do not seem to be plotting to make us happy. Most are very pleasant. Some are unusual. A few are downright difficult.

Every person is different; each has a unique personality. But the kind of people who tend to bug us the most are the ones who are not like us. Accept this diversity and learn to enjoy it. Know that people's needs are basically the same at some level and that treating them as guests will create the most goodwill, most of the time.

Work on verbal discipline: Train your self-talk and your comments to others to focus on the positive, and avoid being judgmental. Instead of saying, "Can you believe that ugly dress on that lady?" say, "She dresses interestingly." Instead of saying, "This guy will nickel and dime me to death," say "This customer is very cost-conscious."

At times you'll have to force yourself to avoid the negative and judgmental, but accept the challenge and you can make a game out of it.

Here is a challenge: Sincerely try for one full day to *avoid saying anything negative or judgmental* about another person. If you make it through the day, shoot for another day. Verbal discipline can become a habit that pays off.

You'll find yourself enjoying people more.

To build on a good start

11. Call people by name

A person's name is his favorite sound. We appreciate it when people make the effort to find out our names and use them in addressing us. When appropriate, introduce yourself to the customer and ask his name. If this isn't appropriate (such as when you are waiting on a line of customers) you can often get the customer's name from his check, credit card, order form or other paperwork.

But don't be overly familiar too quickly. You are normally safe calling people Mr. Smith or Ms. Jones but may be seen as rude if you call them Homer or Marge. (This is especially true when younger employees are dealing with older customers.) Better to err on the side of being too formal. If people prefer first-name address, they'll tell you so.

12. Listen with more than your ears

Since so few people are really good listeners, this skill provides an excellent *E-Plus* opportunity.

There is no such thing as an unpopular listener. Almost everyone becomes more interesting when they stop talking. Pay attention to your talk-listen ratio. Are you giving the customer at least equal time?

To be a better listener, use these ideas:

- *Judge the content* of what people are saying, *not the way they are saying it*. Customers may not have the "right" words, but they know what they need better than anyone.

- *Hold your fire.* Don't jump to make judgments before your customer has finished talking.

- *Work at listening.* Maintain eye contact and discipline yourself to listen to what is being said. Tune out those thoughts that get you thinking about something else.

- *Resist distractions.* Make the customer the center of your attention.

- *Seek clarification* from customers so you fully understand their needs. Do this in a nonthreatening way using sincere, open-ended questions.

13. Anticipate customer needs

Helen, a middle-aged woman, was hired to work in a local department store during the Christmas season. During a particularly hectic day, a young pregnant mother with two toddlers holding onto her approached Helen's cash register. Spotting the woman, Helen excused herself from the other customers for a moment and took a chair from behind the counter to the young woman.

"Why don't you sit down here?" she asked, "And I'll ring up your purchases in a few minutes and bring them back to you."

The shopper was astounded and appreciative! Her expectations were definitely exceeded!

All Helen did was *anticipate customer needs* and then do something about them. She won a loyal customer for that store through her initiative and good sense.

(Incidentally, this illustration speaks well for hiring middle-aged women, especially women who have withstood the demands of raising a family. They tend to be empathetic and creative.)

Other ways we might anticipate and meet needs:

- *Be sure the customer has everything needed* to use the product. (If he buys paint, for example, ask if he has enough brushes, thinner, sandpaper, etc.)

- *Offer to carry merchandise* to the customer's car or deliver it to his home or office.

- *Respond to the customer's urgency.* If he's in a hurry, work quickly to accommodate. Failing to share such urgency can convey a disinterested attitude.

- *Help reduce confusion.* If an application form is difficult, show your customer which parts he needs to complete and you can fill in the rest.

- *Be sure your customer has enough information* to use the product or service. (If written directions or clarification would be useful, write them and provide photocopies to customers.)

Again, the theme here is to exceed your customers' expectations. Provide just a little more than they might expect from you or businesses like yours.

14. Reach out and touch them

Physical touch is a powerful form of communication. Take an opportunity to shake hands with a customer or even pat him on the back, if appropriate.

A study of bank tellers shows the power of touch. Tellers were taught to place change in the hand of the customer rather than place it on the counter. Researchers found that customer perceptions of the bank rose sharply among customers who had been touched. In a similar study, servers who touched their restaurant customers when giving change or a receipt found their tips increased dramatically.

To add sincerity to a handshake, use the "Dolly Madison" approach: Place your left hand over their right when gripping in a handshake.

Among internal customers and co-workers, a literal pat on the back can build instant rapport. But don't overdo it; some people resent people who seem too "touchy-feely."

Recognize different preferences; try touching behavior but be willing to adjust if the person seems uncomfortable or ill at ease.

15. Compliment freely and sincerely

It only takes a second and can add enormous goodwill. Say something complimentary to your customers. Safe ground for sincere compliments:

- *Some article of clothing they are wearing.* ("I like that tie," or "That's a beautiful sweater you have on.")

To build on a good start

- *Their children.* ("Your little boy is really cute," or "How old is your daughter? She's beautiful.")
- *Their behavior.* ("Thanks for waiting. You've been very patient," or "I noticed you checking the ____. You're a careful shopper.")
- *Something they own.* ("I like your car. What year is it?" or "I noticed your championship ring. Did you play on that team?")

To get yourself in the habit of complimenting, try this: Set a goal to give 10 sincere compliments each day. Make it a habit and you'll see a sharp increase in your personal popularity. People love to be complimented.

16. Fish for negative feedback

Complaining customers can be your best friends. Without their expressing problems, you could never know how to improve. Without improvement, you would stagnate and eventually fail. (In customer service there is no neutral gear. You either improve or slip backward.)

The best ways to get feedback are:

- Let customers know that you really want their honest opinions (good news or bad).
- Provide ways for them to tell you.

We can get such feedback in several ways but the simplest is *naive listening*. This uses open-ended questions to let people express their ideas. An open-ended question is one that cannot be answered with a simple yes, no or one-word response.

Below are some common questions you hear every day in businesses that can be easily changed to open-ended:

- "Was everything okay?" can become, "How was your food?"
- "Can I get you something else?" can become, "What desserts would you like to order?"
- "Will that be all?" can become, "How else might we serve you today?"

In each of these examples, the second question (the open-ended one) creates an opportunity for customers to express their thoughts in their own words.

Open up the communication channels, and give your customers opportunities to suggest ways they'd like to see you do business. Make it easy to *complain*. Why?

Because 63 percent of unhappy customers who do not complain will *not* buy from you again. But, of those who do complain and have their problems resolved, only five percent will not come back.

There are two main reasons people do not complain when they are dissatisfied:

- They think their complaints will do no good.
- They aren't sure how to voice their complaints.

Your job is to show that complaints do make a difference (by letting them know when problems they point out have been corrected) and to make it easy for them to complain.

Ask for feedback, take it seriously, don't be overly defensive about "the way we've always done it" and express appreciation to the customer for pointing out the problem.

You'll never know about your customers' expectations—and whether you are exceeding them—until you get that needed feedback.

17. Watch your timing

Nothing impresses so significantly as immediate follow-through. Successful salespeople follow up with customers (usually by phone) to see that their purchases are satisfactory. Some salespeople do this occasionally when they have a little spare time; the more successful do it regularly at scheduled times. Likewise, the best customer-oriented people outside of sales make commitments to customers and *always follow up*.

What can you do to improve timing and follow-up in your organization?

A simple form can help you follow up with customers and avoid the possibility of commitments dropping through the cracks. Make up your form in a notebook or on separate sheets. Include these four columns:

Customer follow-up form

Date	Commitment (name, phone number, what you promised)	Due	Done

18. Explain how things work

An automobile sales rep surprised me—*E-Plussed* me—when I bought my last car. He took about 45 minutes showing me all the features of the car and how to work every one of them. It was like going through the owner's manual, page by page—but much easier and more pleasant.

Solidify your customers by ensuring that they will have no problems with the products they buy. Take a moment to explain how things work and what to look out for in using them. Create clear expectations about what the product can deliver.

If your product is a service, show customers how to maintain the results or continue getting benefits from it. If they will receive something in the mail, tell them when. If a follow-up action is necessary, explain how it will be arranged.

19. Reassure the decision to do business with you

Buyer's remorse can set in pretty fast, especially when people make large purchases. At the time of sale, you can inoculate against remorse by reassuring the customer that she's made a good purchasing decision.

Phrases like, "I'm sure you'll get many hours of enjoyment out of this," or "Your family will love it" can help reassure and strengthen the buyer's resolve to follow through with the purchase and feel good about it.

A government agency might say, "I'll bet you're glad this is over with for another year," or "I'll handle the renewal—you've done all that is necessary."

A powerful tool for reassuring is the telephone. One consulting approach for bank executives shows how important customer calls can be. As part of a training session, the executives develop a simple script and immediately go to the phones to call some of their customers. The conversation goes something like this:

"Hello, I'm Chris Wilson from Major Bank. I just wanted to call to let you know that we appreciate your business and would be interested in any suggestions you might have for additional ways we could serve you."

Then they let the customer talk. The results: Customers are astounded that their banker would actually call and that he wasn't trying to sell anything! The image of the bank's service goes up sharply.

20. Under-promise, over-deliver

Constantly look for ways you can give customers a little more than they expect. That's the essence of *E-Plus*. Look at how some major companies use this principle:

A well-known air freight company claims to deliver your package by 10:00 a.m. the next morning, but often delivers it by 9:00 or 9:30. The repair office for a major office equipment company makes it a point to have the service person arrive earlier than promised. A successful repairman often charges the customer a few dollars *less* than estimated.

What can you do to over-deliver? Here are some ideas:

• *Provide it faster.*

- *Offer to deliver it.* ("I'll drop it by your house on my way home this evening.")
- *Offer to handle the transaction efficiently.* ("You just fill in this part and I'll handle the rest.")
- *Take a trade-in* (or dispose of the old one).
- *Offer to handle additional paperwork.* ("I'll get the license forms taken care of for you.")

Use your imagination. And remember: Exceeding expectations is the single most powerful way to build customer loyalty.

To save a possible loss

21. Master recovery skills

Only you can be the judge of whether a customer is worth saving, but if you read the beginning of this book, you'll recognize the tremendous cost of replacing a customer. So why not try to save the ones you have? To do so, use "recovery" skills.

Recognize that upset customers want some or all of the following from you:

- To be listened to and taken seriously.
- To have you understand the problem and the reason they are upset.
- To receive compensation or restitution.
- To get the problem handled quickly.
- To avoid further inconvenience.
- To be treated with respect.
- To have someone punished for the problem.
- To be assured that the problem will not happen again.

If all goes well, you should feel a genuine sense of satisfaction after handling an unhappy or irate customer. But this is not a perfect world and people are not always rational, so sometimes you, too, get upset.

The key things to remember are:

- If you have *tried your best to satisfy* the customer, you have done all that you can do.
- Don't take it personally. Upset people often say things they don't mean. They are blowing off steam, venting frustration. If the problem was your fault, resolve to learn from the experience and do better next time. If you had no control over the situation, do what you can to make things better, but don't bat your head against the wall.
- *Don't rehash the experience* with your co-workers or in your mind. What's done is done. Recounting the experience with others probably won't make their day any better and it will just make you mad. You may, however, want to ask another person how they would have handled the situation.
- Use every customer contact experience as an *opportunity to improve* your professionalism. The most unpleasant encounter can teach us useful lessons.

When the situation has cooled, you may want to review with an eye toward improving your skills.

Think back on the situation where you used your recovery skills and ask questions like these:

- What was the nature of the complaint?
- How did the customer see the problem? Who was to blame, what irritated him most, why was he angry or frustrated?
- How did you see the problem? Was the customer partially to blame?
- What did you say to the customer that seemed to help the situation? What did you say that seemed to aggravate the situation?

- How did you show your concern to the customer?
- How did you apply your communication skills?
- How did you demonstrate your competence?
- What would you do differently?
- Do you think this customer will do business with you again? Why or why not?

22. Disarm the chronic complainer

"Stubbornness is the energy of fools," says a German proverb. Sometimes we need to draw the line between upset customers with legitimate problems and chronic complainers who consume our time with unreasonable demands—the dreaded "customers from hell."

Step one in dealing with such people is to *be sure* you've got a *chronic* complainer.

When you've tried the normal recovery approaches and nothing seems to work, look for the following telltale signs:[5]

- *He always looks for someone to blame.* In his world there is no such thing as an accident: Someone is always at fault, and it is probably you.

- *He never admits any degree of fault or responsibility.* He sees himself as a blameless victim of the incompetence or malice of others.

---

[5] Adapted from "How to Deal With Those Chronic Complainers," in *Customer Service Manager's Letter*, September 20, 1989. Published by Prentice-Hall Professional Newsletters. The article is based on the work of Dr. Robert Bramson, *Coping With Difficult People* (New York: Dell, 1988).

- *He has strong ideas about what others should do.* He loves to define other people's duties. If you hear a complaint phrased in terms of what other people always, never, must or must not do, chances are you're talking to a chronic complainer.
- *He complains at length.* While a normal complainer pauses for breath every now and then, a chronic seems able to inhale while saying the words, "and another thing..."

When faced with the occasional chronic complainer (they are quite rare, fortunately), try these techniques:

- *Active listening* to identify the legitimate grievance. Rephrase the complaint in your own words, even if you have to interrupt to do so. Say something like, "Excuse me, but do I understand you to say that the package didn't arrive on time and you feel frustrated and annoyed?"
- *Establish the facts* to reduce the complainer's tendency to exaggerate or overgeneralize. If he says he tried calling all day, establish the actual number of times called and when.
- *Resist the temptation to apologize,* although it may seem the natural thing to do. Since the complainer is trying to fix blame—not solve problems—your apology will be seen as an invitation to further blaming. Instead, ask questions like, "Would an extended warranty solve your problem?" or "When is the best time for me to call you back with the information you requested?"
- *Force the complainer to pose solutions* to the problem, especially if he doesn't seem to like your ideas. Also, try putting a time limit on the conversation by saying something like, "I have

to talk with someone in 10 minutes. What sort of action plan can we work out in that time?" The object of this is to get him away from whining and into a problem-solving mode.

There are, of course, no guarantees when dealing with such customers, but the effort may well be worth it. Converting one of these folks into a normal, rational customer can be professionally rewarding.

23. Tell how you fixed it

Customer relations is a subcategory of public relations and the first rule of public relations is: *Let good deeds be noticed.* If you fix a customer's problem, tell that customer, and in some cases, tell other customers too.

Follow-up calls to repair customers to be sure that their problems have been solved (even if you know they have been) remind them that you care.

Example: An auto service department replaced my car's radio immediately rather than removing it and sending it off for repair. The service manager said he didn't want me to be "driving around with a hole in my dashboard" like other dealers might have me do. This served as a reminder that he'd given me good service.

24. Reconcile with *E-Plus*

Remember, *E-Plus* means *exceeding* customer expectations. When attempting to recover an unhappy customer, the icing on the cake is the "something extra" you give by way of making up for the problem.

Suppose you buy a new pair of shoes and the heel falls off. You call the shoe store and the owner tells you to bring them back for replacement. You take an hour off from work, drive downtown to the store and battle for a parking space. He cheerfully gives you a new pair of shoes. Are you satisfied now?

Probably not. Why? Because he really hasn't repaid you for the inconvenience. Sure, he stood behind the product and perhaps even did so in a pleasant manner, but you still came out short.

What kinds of things can we do to apply the *E-Plus* idea? What would be seen as going the extra mile in the eyes of the customer? Some of these may work:

- *Offer to pick up or deliver* goods to be replaced or repaired.
- *Give a gift* of merchandise to repay for the inconvenience. The gift may be small but the thought will be appreciated.
- *Reimburse* for the cost of returning the merchandise such as parking fees, etc. (Mail-order retailers pay all return postage fees in order to reduce customer annoyance and inconvenience.)
- *Acknowledge* the customer's inconvenience and thank him for coming back.

Section III

Powerful Ideas Managers Can Use

To create a climate of caring

25. Get everyone involved in setting a theme

As I consult with organizations, I typically ask if they have a customer service theme or credo. Fairly often I get answers something like this: "Oh, yes, we have 13 points to excellent customer service."

I'd reply, "Oh, really? What's point 11?" The manager would say, "Well, I don't know exactly." Then I'd ask, "Well, how about point 6? Which one's that?" And he would say, "I'm not sure, I actually haven't memorized all of them, but they are posted around the office."

That's not good enough for today's competitive environment. Identifying a theme means coming up with a succinct, clear statement of what the organization is about and how it could be seen as unique in the eyes of the customer.

Let's go through that one more time. An effective credo or theme must be:

- Succinct.
- Clear.
- Unique.

The reason you want it succinct and clear is so that every employee can remember and "buy into" this as a guiding statement that will shape her actions and help her make decisions.

Let's look at a couple of examples.

- One well-respected customer service organization is Federal Express, the package delivery service. Do they have a simple, clear theme? Yes they do: "Absolutely, positively, overnight." They will get the packages there absolutely, positively, overnight, and they're 99.8 percent successful at doing that.

- A *Harvard Business Review*[6] article told of a Seattle restaurant staff who wrestled with the idea of a simple, clear theme. After carefully looking at the company through the eyes of their customers and deciding what the restaurant guests wanted from them, they came up with this theme: "Your enjoyment guaranteed. Always." That's exactly what they offer their guests, enjoyment.

A neat thing about this simple theme was that people could buy into it, and in fact they made it into an acronym: YEGA. While YEGA may not mean anything to most of us, it became a catch word for their organization. They developed YEGA promotions and YEGA bucks and YEGA pins and hats to get their employees involved in the spirit of YEGA. It was fun, it was interesting and it reminded the employees constantly of that simple four-word theme: "Your enjoyment guaranteed. Always."

---

[6] See Timothy W. Firnstahl, "My Employees Are My Service Guarantee," *Harvard Business Review*, July-August 1989, pp. 28-32.

Here is how to articulate a good theme:

- *Commit* to working on the process of identifying a theme.

- *Make it succinct, clear and unique.*

- *Gather ideas from your customers.* Ask them, "What five things do you want as customers in doing business with us?" Ask them to respond quickly off the tops of their heads, and look at the language they use.

- Similarly, gather your own people together in the organization and ask, "If you were our customer, what five things would you like to get from a company like ours?" Ask people to respond quickly and then collect all of the words.

As you gather perceptions from customers and employees, you'll notice that some terms come up over and over again. These typically are the kinds of words that will reassure your customer. These are good words to put into your customer service theme.

As you draft a theme for your organization, remember:

- Participation and input from customers and employees is very important. The customers can best tell you what they're looking for in an organization like yours, and the employees' participation will ensure they will accept the theme.

- Write several rough drafts of the theme; don't be too quick to come up with the finished version. Phrase the final version in 10 words or fewer.

- If possible, try to make the theme into an acronym, where the first letters of each word form a word in themselves. For example, one computer company launched a program called CARE which stood for "Customers Are Really Everything." The YEGA example I gave earlier is another example of an acronym.

When you've identified a statement of uniqueness, ask yourself the question, "Would everyone in the organization choose roughly the same words we've chosen to describe this distinctiveness?"

A simple way to verify this is to ask some of your employees to describe the organization's theme. Especially, invite an employee who's been with the organization for 10 days or less to identify the theme.

What good does it do just to be able to repeat such a phrase? Repeating some words may seem meaningless at first, but most organizations fall far short even of that level of agreement. Focusing your people on a common theme is well worth the effort.

Tom Peters, in his book, *Thriving on Chaos*, says that this kind of a statement of "what we are" has to meet the following criteria. It has to be:

• Roughly right.
• Enduring.
• Succinct.
• Memorable.
• Believable.
• Energizing to all.

One final note: A theme is not necessarily forever. As an organization changes directions as markets or economic conditions change, a theme may be modified. Some organizations may want to use their theme statements for a limited period of time much the way advertisers use specific slogans for only a few years.

Modifying the theme should not, however, be done without careful thought. Consistency of direction is in itself valuable.

Important: By having employees participate in clarifying a theme, they will feel more committed to it. This has been shown time and again since the earliest studies in human relations.

Front line people know the customers best and can give great ideas on how to better serve them. Never overlook the ideas of this group of experts. The employees on the firing line have the best ideas. Use them.

26. Reward the right actions

Fairly often, organizations inadvertently reward one behavior while hoping for something else. In all too many cases an organization hopes something will happen but actually rewards an opposite behavior.

For example: A company rewards individuals and departments for never receiving complaints. The hope is that by receiving no complaints it means we are doing a good job. The reality, however, may well be that no complaints are heard because the complaints are simply being suppressed. Customers have no effective way to voice complaints. Instead, they just quit doing business with the company.

As we discussed earlier, it's not bad news to receive a complaint, but it *is* bad news to suppress a complaint. Some percentage of customers will always be less than satisfied, and ignoring them does no good. Instead, it makes sense to draw out those customer concerns so that they can be addressed and corrected. As someone once said, "Even the ostrich leaves one end exposed."

Here are some other examples of possible reward conflicts where the wrong behaviors may be rewarded and the right behaviors ignored:

- Rewarding employees for fast transaction handling when the customer may be left uninformed or resent being rushed along. Examples: The restaurant that encourages employees to get the customer fed and out may create unhappy customers who prefer to eat more slowly, or the electronic equipment buyer who does not understand how to work the features of his VCR before she leaves the dealership.

- Encouraging salespeople to "cooperate with each other to best meet the customer needs" while paying a straight commission. Example: Salespeople practically trip over each other to approach the new customer before the other guy gets her.

- Encouraging employees to send thank-you notes to customers but never allowing on-the-job time to do so. This creates the impression that it really isn't that important.

- Constantly stressing the need to reduce the amount of return merchandise by docking the pay of clerks who accept too many returns. Result: Customers encounter reluctance to take back unsatisfactory products.

- Paying people by the hour instead of by the task accomplished. Hourly wages are simpler to administer but they basically pay people for using up time!

Check your organization. Are you really rewarding the right behaviors?

The reward system within an organization needs to be tilted to the advantage of the employee who provides excellent service. Any rewards should be given in direct relationship to the employee's contribution to customer service consistent with the theme you've selected.

Rewards take many forms. Some are obvious, some subtle:

- Salary and cash bonuses.
- Prizes and awards.
- Promotions and job enrichment.
- Preferred work locations, better offices, larger desks.
- Work scheduling flexibility.
- Pins, badges, uniforms.
- Reserved parking spaces.
- "Employee of the week (or month)" recognition.
- Compliments, spoken or written.
- Surprise recognition parties or celebrations.
- Lunches or banquets.
- Newsletter write-ups.

Management is only limited by imagination when it comes to rewarding employees. The most important point is that managers reward the right actions and results.

27. Train and retrain to build employee competence

People quickly forget ideas they have been taught in training sessions. Repeated exposures to the same ideas are almost always necessary for people to apply those ideas. Training cannot be a one-shot affair such as a once-a-year retreat. It must be continuous.

Training need not always be formal classroom sessions. Often the best training happens in small groups or one-to-one communication among associates in an organization.

When I worked as a manager for a public utility, we found the best results occurred when supervisors spent about 10 minutes each morning before opening to the public to remind service representatives of the skills and behaviors they needed to apply. Like a coach warming up a star athlete, the good supervisor trains and retrains on a regular basis.

Remember, training is much more than just telling. It involves hands-on practice, critiques and regular follow-up.

Example: A restaurant assigns an experienced, successful server to "shadow" the newer employee, observing and helping. The newer employee benefits from the critique and the comfort of knowing that the backup can help out if a problem arises. The experienced server feels a sense of contribution from the mini-management role.

How do we know what kind of training to provide?

Employees recognize that most of their tasks fall within their scope of ability, but that in some cases they don't know what to do. To broaden their professional competence, they need to find the answers and try out new skills.

Managers should try to encourage their employees to list questions they have or skills they'd like to sharpen or learn. Have them answer the following question for each the three categories described:

What more information or additional skills would you like to know about...

- *The department's or organization's procedures?*
- *The products and services we sell?*
- *Handling customers effectively?*

Encourage people to share their lists with supervisors and jointly make plans to get the training and experience needed.

Training builds competence. Customers gain a sense of confidence and reassurance as they watch experts at work.

Excellent customer service people work to continually learn and grow. They know how important it is to keep current about their organization, its products, services and procedures. They know that they are ultimately responsible for upgrading their skills and increasing their value and professionalism.

Example: The following situation was written up by the editor of an investment magazine and distributed to thousands of readers.[7] It clearly illustrates the problem of low competence:

> *One day last month I went to buy a cordless drill. At the first store I tried, I was encouraged when I immediately found one that seemed suitable. When I went to pay for it, however, I found that it did not have a price tag. To make matters worse, not a single clerk was in sight.*

---

[7] Written by Susan Feldman, Editor-in-Chief, *Investment Vision*, a publication of Fidelity Investments, 1989.

The author goes on to describe how she overheard a clerk telling another customer that he could probably get the item he wanted from a competitor, and that he could get a discount there as well!

When I asked for help, she said, "Well, that's not really my department," but she finally agreed and spent the next 10 minutes poking through an unruly pile of merchandise that bore not the faintest resemblance to the item I sought.

Later, the department manager came bustling out to help. After more fruitless searching, he offered to sell the writer the sample if she "thought $39.95 was a reasonable price." This caused the writer to wonder:

Shouldn't prices be set by some higher authority, I thought? Didn't barter go out with agrarian societies? Desperate to get out of the store, I agreed.

When she went to the register to pay for the item, the clerk punched in the product code number, and found that the price was $69.95. When the customer said she didn't want the merchandise, the clerk said "Yeah, I don't blame you—too expensive."

And so ended another excruciating hour of shopping at an establishment where the customer comes last.

Contrast that story with one where competence is stressed. A chain of athletic footwear and clothing stores was written up for its efforts to improve competence:

...the company puts all its store managers through a 12-to-18-month, soup-to-nuts training

process. Employees learn about every aspect of the operation from the structure of the foot and the basics of bookkeeping to techniques for closing a sale and selling to children. And that's not all. Each store is also equipped with a VCR, the better to play a series of specialized training videotapes. Store managers also receive sports-medicine books so they can become familiar with the health problems of their customers.[8]

The difference is the emphasis on training and retraining. Where would you rather shop?

28. Explain the taboos in no uncertain terms

Managers should make clear from the first day of employment that there are specific taboos, things that are simply not to be done in the organization. For example, in a supermarket, checkout clerks are told repeatedly of this taboo: They must absolutely avoid chatting with each other about personal matters when a customer is present. This supermarket placed special emphasis on this taboo because it recently reinstated baggers at all the checkout counters. (A few years ago, it was fashionable to have the customers bag their own groceries and thus save a little bit of money. But customers have changed and people now want to have the groceries packaged for them.) The new procedure now calls for two people at

---

[8] From "The Smart Sales Staff," published in *Success*, April 1989.

each cash register, a checker and a bagger. The danger in this is that the checker and the bagger, often young people, enjoy each other's company and may find themselves talking to each other and ignoring the customer. Therefore, management simply told each employee that if there are no customers around it's okay to chat while you're working, but when the customer appears, all personal discussions and chit-chat must stop.

In other organizations, taboos are clearly spelled out, such as:

- Never make fun of a customer.
- Never accept a tip or gratuity from a customer.
- Never respond sarcastically to a customer comment.
- Never sit down on the job.
- Never allow the phone to interrupt a face-to-face conversation with a customer.
- Never degrade a competitor's product, a customer's trade-in, a customer's expressed preference, etc.

Taboos are the "shalt not's" of customer service. Keep the list of taboos reasonably short, but be sure they are consistently enforced.

29. Rescue your people from unreasonable customers

It comes with the territory. Managers are expected to handle the customer that can't be handled by employees. The manager serves as backup. The heavy hitter. The fixer. She can do it all and her people will be watching how she handles the tough nut. (For specific ideas on handling the chronic complainer, see Idea #22.) Remember the advice of Will Rogers who said, "Diplomacy is the art of saying 'nice doggie' until you can find a rock."

People you work with will appreciate your willingness to rescue them from unreasonable customers. So keep your people skills sharp. Learn how to better communicate and deal with different kinds of people. Read books on the subject; attend seminars. Keep developing your professionalism.

30. Give your people a break

Las Vegas dealers work 20-minute shifts. How long do your people work with customers?

Customer contact work can be some of the most emotionally demanding labor imaginable. To stay sharp and do it right, people need breaks. Especially when things are hectic, try to schedule a break or a diversion (perhaps other work that gets them away from customers) regularly.

No one can keep totally cool indefinitely. To paraphrase Vince Lombardi, "Fatigue makes cowards (and grouches!) of us all."

31. Provide the right stuff

Be sure your people have the tools to do the job. Can everyone who needs one find:

• A telephone in a place where it can be heard?
• A computer with customer records?

- A fax machine or messenger service?
- Letterhead, envelopes, postage?
- Business cards?
- Product information and publications?
- Policy statements?
- A desk, writing table or place to confer with customers?
- Office supplies?
- A mobile or portable phone?

Customer service to meet today's challenges needs today's equipment.

32. Know where to recruit

Steal good employees. As you come across people with a great attitudes and excellent customer service skills, try to hire them away or at least recommend them to your boss. Start a file of people you'd like to have working for you and when an opening occurs, contact them.

Don't worry if they are working in a totally different type of business. The specifics of your organization can be taught. Great attitudes cannot.

To grow service champions

33. Nurture a culture of caring

What is a culture? It's a whole set of values, attitudes and ways of doing things that are generally accepted by organization leaders and members. The culture defines rules of behavior, written and unwritten, that employees are expected to live by. Without such a set of rules and norms, an employee becomes confused and ineffective, like a foreigner driving an automobile in a strange country. Ignorance of the rules inevitably leads to mistakes or violations.

An organization's culture is not something that can be "put in place" by decree. A culture emerges over a period of time. Don't try to rush the process.

To use the power of customer service, an organization needs to develop and nurture a culture that really cares about customers. To do that, several factors are necessary:

- Top management support.
- The long view—patience.
- Employee involvement.
- Ongoing training.
- Rewards that reinforce the right behaviors.
- Taboos.
- Hoopla and fun.

79

Managers, how do your organizations measure up? Do your people have a sense of the culture? If not, start discussions with them to help articulate these necessary factors.

34. Enrich people's jobs

As we reward appropriate behaviors and carefully observe what people are doing, we start to grow service champions, people who become real advocates of their customers.

The best indicator of whether a person is a service champion is viewing who they are working for. Given the choice, you are better off with someone who works first for the customer and second for the company. These people are your champions. This isn't really an either-or choice; serving the customer *is* serving the company, so long as these employees don't give away the store.

Managers need to recognize champion potential and cultivate it. Here are some ways to identify and grow potential champs:

- *Look for people with "task maturity,"* that is, they have good potential business sense. *Note:* This kind of maturity has nothing to do with age. Instead, it results from the individual's:

  1. Ability to set ambitious but attainable goals.
  2. Willingness and capability to take responsibility for his results and actions.
  3. Experience and/or education relevant to the job he is doing.
  4. Personal self-confidence, self-respect and general good judgment.

People with these characteristics become the best candidates for growth on the job.

- *Give the "mature" employee additional authority* to act on behalf of the customer. Example: The company previously had a blanket rule that any refunds over $10 must be approved by a manager. Allow service champions to handle their own approvals. Other areas where the "mature" employee may be given additional authority might be:
  1. Approving unusual orders or exceptions to the "normal" customer requests.
  2. Authorizing home delivery of merchandise or pickup of defective products.
  3. Approving checks or other methods of payment.
  4. Scheduling work times, breaks and lunch hours.
  5. Making unsolicited customer follow-up calls.
  6. Suggesting different compensation, bonus systems or special promotions.
  7. Participation in merchandise buying decisions.
  8. Monitoring or training newer employees.

These and other forms of job enrichment build service champions by rewarding them with additional job freedom and opportunities to take initiative.

When employees truly feel free to be advocates for their customers, they begin to give exemplary service that goes beyond what the customers expect.

35. Take the long view

Just as the impact of one lost customer is not felt immediately, the impact of an ongoing improvement program takes time to mature. Recognizing that a lost customer is not just a few dollars a week in income, but thousands or tens of thousands of dollars over a period of years, is one example of the long view.

Another example: Recognizing the psychological cost of unhappy customers on employees. People working with disgruntled and, in some cases, outraged customers day after day pay a terrible cost in terms of stress and job dissatisfaction. While the impact may not be immediate, by taking the long view we soon recognize the costs in employee attitudes, health, absenteeism and eventual turnover.

Changing employee behavior takes time. Changing customer perceptions of an organization takes longer. Service improvement programs need to be phased in and stuck with even though they don't appear to bear immediate fruit.

Example: When organizations tackle a particular customer problem, they may, by digging into the nature of the problem, find that things seem to get worse: They receive *more* complaints and more dissatisfied customers initially. This is not a deteriorating situation, but the outcome of better measurements of the extent of the problem.

As the company improves methods and employee behaviors, the number of customer complaints drops. This drop is a real improvement, not an illusion created by burying heads in the sand.

36. Recognize and reinforce

Catch your people doing things right. Also, let them know they've been caught!

For too long, managers have focused on catching mistakes and jumping down the throats of those who commit them. The problem with such an approach is that it focuses on exactly the wrong thing. Here's why: What we focus on grows—we get more of it. If a manager keeps looking for screw-ups, he or she will find more and more of them. It gets frustrating.

If, instead, we want good customer behaviors to grow in our organizations, focus on the positive things happening. Then reinforce the positive behaviors caught.

Don't underestimate the power of simple rewards. Nothing is so powerful as verbal reinforcement given appropriately and in a timely manner. If your people are doing the kinds of things you want them to be doing—they are serving the customers in appropriate and exemplary ways—they need to be thanked and appreciated.

In catching people doing things right and rewarding those behaviors, we create a sense of pride in the organization. People will feel better about their jobs and will be more likely to stick with the company.

Managers have often misunderstood what is actually rewarding to employees. A recent national survey asked workers to state what they wanted most from their jobs in order of importance. At the same time, managers were asked to state their guesses of what the employees would find most important. Here are the surprising results:[9]

---

[9] From Jack Weissman Associates as quoted in *Customer Service Manager's Letter*, (a Prentice-Hall Professional Newsletter), September 6, 1989.

Job factors that matter most to employees

	Manager's Guess	Worker's Rating
1. Appreciation for good work	8	1
2. Feeling "in" on things	10	2
3. Help with personal problems	9	3
4. Job security	2	4
5. Good wages	1	5
6. Interesting work	5	6
7. Possibility for promotion	3	7
8. Personal loyalty to company/boss	6	8
9. Good working conditions	4	9
10. Tactful discipline	7	10

What does this have to do with catching and rewarding? It suggests that what have traditionally been regarded as rewards may be only a small portion of the available reinforcers managers can use.

The single, most effective way to reward workers is to tell them how much you appreciate what they do. To give such compliments impact, make them:

- *Direct and specific.* Address them personally and tell them why you are pleased with what they've done: Example: "Tom, you did a really nice job of handling that situation with Mrs. Burton. I think she feels good about us and will probably be back as a customer. Thanks." Or: "Brenda, you did a really good job of picking up on that customer's disappointment. Most people would have just let her go unhappy, but you sensed that something was wrong and you fixed it. That's great customer service. Thanks."

- *Unconditionally positive.* Don't slip in a "left-handed compliment" or any comment that diminishes the praise. Avoid: "Marge, you sure handled Mr. Johnson's problem nicely—for once you actually sold him something, too!" Or: "You kept your cool, Don. Those anti-depressant drugs must be working for you. Keep up the good work." Or: "Nice sale, Harry. Can we talk about your order screw-up after lunch?"

Awareness of what employees want in their jobs helps managers create other forms of reward. For example, the study mentioned that workers want to feel "in" on things. A form of reward for great customer service, then, might be to invite a worker to serve on a decision-making committee (be sure this isn't just additional work piled on top of what he's already expected to do). Or, simply confiding in the worker about future plans can be rewarding. Example: "Ron, you seem to have a real feel for what the customers expect from us. I'd appreciate you reaction to this idea we've been kicking around about a home-delivery service. Would you help us think this through?"

While it is important to let your people know when they've been caught doing things right, we don't always know. Managers cannot be everywhere. Heroic deeds may often go virtually unnoticed despite best efforts to recognize and reward. And sometimes, it's difficult to adequately reinforce people during the heat of the battle.

Two approaches to delivering reinforcement have been used by companies. Both involve giving employees a card or "coupon" to let them know their work has been recognized.

Example: Circle K convenience stores printed cards (the size of a standard business card) with "The Circle K

Corporation 5 Commandments" printed on one side and, on the back side, the following:

CONGRATULATIONS

You have just been caught using
the "5 commandments."

| Signature | Title | Date |

On the top line, the giver of the card fills in the name of the employee; the manager also signs and dates the card.

Such cards are then sent to the corporate offices where they can be exchanged for gifts and prizes.

A few years ago, American Airlines did a similar promotion making coupons available to their regular customers (frequent flyers). The cards could be given to any AA employee who performed exemplary service. Again, the coupons were redeemed for prizes. (If your organization has a regular customer base, an approach that allows the customers to pass out the "rewards" is particularly effective.)

37. Track customer service behaviors over time

It's important to keep track of observations over a period of time to create an ongoing emphasis on service excellence. Without ongoing measures and tracking, customer service becomes no more than a short-term "program."

Among the observations that could be tracked are:

• Average scores received on shopper surveys.

• Number of customer complaints received and handled.

• Number of company-initiated calls to customers to assess satisfaction.

• Office accessibility (how many times customers experience busy signals or long lines).

• Random[10] observations of employee behaviors. Count such things as eye contact time, smiling, efficiency of handling transactions, courtesy, thanking customers, etc.

38. Use hoopla and fun

People enjoy working in organizations that are fun. Many organizations have regular rituals, whether they be Friday afternoon popcorn, birthday parties or employee of the month celebrations, that everyone gets involved in. In the 1982 classic management book, *In Search of Excellence*, Tom Peters and Robert Waterman talk about the importance of hoopla and fun. Excellent organizations are fun places to work, they create rituals of their own.

---

[10] Note the term "random" does not mean haphazard. Carefully plan such measurements so that every employee has an equal chance of being observed.

As a manager at a utility company, I initiated frequent sales contests, complete with skits and prizes. Each time a particular product was sold, the service representative could pop a balloon and find inside of that balloon a prize ranging from a $10 bill to a coupon good for a piece of pie in the company cafeteria. Employees loved it and got involved.

Other ideas:

- Employee (or hero) of the week/month recognition.
- Awards luncheons (include some tongue-in-cheek "awards").
- Win a day off with pay.
- Casual dress days.
- Halloween costume day.
- Family picnics.

39. Create explorer groups

When you hear about a great idea another business is using, send out an exploration party to scope it out.

One supermarket known for exceptional service encourages employees to take a company van and rush to the scene of good service given by others. They take notes and discuss possible implementation in their store.

Other explorer groups can be customers or employees who report their findings to management. Be open to these ideas. Keep your eyes and ears open for new ideas. Sometimes they come from the most unlikely sources.

To tie the customer to the company

40. Create user groups

Some computer stores tie customers to the business by creating user groups. Customers are encouraged and supported in their efforts to share ideas about and uses for their computers and software packages. The store offers a place to meet and publicity via a newsletter.

A store selling cosmetics or health care products might hold makeover classes or physical fitness seminars. Sewing supply stores and craft supply retailers offer classes and establish repeat customers. Medical clinics and mental health facilities sponsor support group meetings and informational seminars.

Many other businesses could benefit from similar groups, but often don't think of it or follow through.

41. Use focus groups

Focus groups have long been used for marketing research but they can also play an exceptionally important role in understanding and managing customer expectations. Although some marketing consultants may disagree, there's no great mystery to how focus groups work and any intelligent person could run one effectively.

Powerful Ideas to Keep Your Customers

Here is the procedure:

- Select a random sample of your customers or patrons to join with you in a feedback sharing session. Don't pick just people you know or customers you like. You may, however, want to be sure they are among your better customers by qualifying them according to how much they spend with you. You can get customers' names off their checks or credit cards or whatever other records you have.

- Formally invite the customers to participate, telling them when and where as well as how long the session will take. Let them know the reason: that you are attempting to better understand customer needs and how you can better be of service to them.

- Keep your focus group to about a dozen people. Ask customers to confirm their attendance but expect that some will not show up. Fifteen confirmed reservations will generally get you 12 actual participants. If you use a mailed invitation, follow up with a phone call.

- Reward focus group participants. Tell those invited that you will give them something for their participation. Retail stores may give focus group participants a gift certificate, a free dinner or even cash. In marketing research, it's not uncommon to pay people $50 dollars or more for a one-or-two-hour session.

One supermarket I worked with was so excited about the focus groups that they invited 40 or 50 people every month! The problem, of course, is that a group that large makes it hard for all people to be heard. Some people dominated the group while others, who had equally good ideas but were uncomfortable speaking before so many people, suppressed their ideas.

To get the most from focus groups:

- Set the stage by having someone from top management moderate the group.

- Create an open atmosphere where participants will feel comfortable giving you all kinds of feedback. Be polite, open, encouraging and receptive.

- Don't ever cut people off when they're making critical comments.

- Do not, above all, be defensive of the way you're doing things now, when in the eyes of the customer it's not working.

- Apply the principle of naive listening. Keep any follow-up questions open-ended.

- When receiving compliments, make a statement such as, "Although we're happy to hear some compliments from you occasionally, our major purpose here is to identify ways that we can do a better job in meeting your needs." As focus group members express compliments, these should be acknowledged and thanked. However the emphasis needs to be on where changes could be made to better meet the needs of the customers.

- Limit the group to a predetermined amount of time. People need to know how long they are expected to stay. Typically a one-hour or (maximum) 90-minute session works best. Any longer than that and you start losing people's interest.

- Tape-record the entire focus group session and transcribe key notes for review. As you analyze the results of this group session, look for key words that might tip you off as to what the customers are looking for. If, for example, concerns about the amount of time needed to complete their transactions comes up repeatedly, you might make the mental note of how your company can best meet customer needs more quickly.

- At the end of the focus group session, be sure to thank the participants for all of their input.

42. Correspond regularly

An athletic shoe store and a rental car agency are good examples of this simple idea. A week after purchasing some running shoes, customers receive a handwritten note from the store owner simply thanking them for buying. No fancy prose, it expresses appreciation for their business and invites them to return.

An airport car rental agency has employees write thank-you notes to customers when the desk is not busy. The notes are handwritten and personalized to mention the type of car rented. They thank the customer and invite them to rent again the next time they are in town.

Don't let your customer forget you

Another way to not let customers forget you is to send them information about upcoming sales, changes in policies, new promotions, etc. Keep the customer tied in. Discount coupons or special hours for preferred customers are often appreciated.

A print shop sends all customers a monthly package of coupons, flyers and samples including a printed quotation on parchment paper suitable for framing. Additional copies of the quote are available free for the asking. The mailing acts as a reminder of the quality of work the shop can do as well as a promotion.

43. Ask often: "How'm I doing?"

Former New York City mayor Ed Koch would constantly ask his constituents, "How'm I doing?" There is some evidence that he even listened to their answers. After all, he was mayor of the Big Apple for many years.

Businesses need to ask that question as many ways as possible. In addition to the measuring and feedback ideas discussed, we need to harbor an attitude of receptiveness.

Being receptive to the comments and criticisms of people is challenging and, at times, frustrating. It takes a lot of courage not only to accept criticism but to actually request it!

Nevertheless, some of your best ideas come from the correction others give you.

44. Make 'em feel special

Customers like to feel important. You can enhance that feeling by:

- Calling them by name. (You can get names from checks, credit cards, application forms or just by asking.)
- Listening to their needs, wants and criticisms.
- Learning their preferences and responding to them. ("Do you still prefer ___?" lets them know that you remember.)

- Getting to know them as people. (Know something about their family, profession, interests, etc.)
- Complimenting and reassuring them.
- Keeping in touch.
- Taking customers' pictures. (An auto agency takes photos of customers with their new cars and posts them on a board. What better way to bring them into the "family of happy customers?")

In short: Treat them like guests you care about. There is no great mystery to such customer care. It's no more than good etiquette, a sense of caring and common sense.

Section IV

Powerful Ideas Salespeople Can Use

To build customer satisfaction and loyalty

45. Explain features and benefits

A feature of your product is simply some aspect of your product. For example, an automobile may have a V-8 engine; a vacuum cleaner may have a hose attachment; a photocopier may copy on both sides of a sheet of paper.

But a benefit is a "what this means to you, the customer" statement. The V-8 engine means you'll have *plenty of pulling power* for your trailer. The hose attachment gets into corners and *makes your home cleaner and more attractive*. The photocopier allows you to *save on paper and postage* since it copies on both sides.

One of the best examples of a benefit statement was seen on a box that holds attachments for a vacuum cleaner. There written in large letters: "More free time for you." It didn't say, "This machine really sucks up the dirt," or "Your house will be cleaner." It got to the ultimate benefit, more free time.

Take some time to rethink the features and benefits of your products or services. Make a long list of them. Really reach for those benefit statements. Remember, a benefit statement tells the customer what the feature means to him or her.

Using benefit statements results in more sales and happier customers.

46. Go for the add-on sales

Often our service position gives an opportunity to anticipate and meet customer needs with add-on sales. This isn't high-pressure selling. It can be a real service to your customer.

Examples: A shoe salesperson asks customers if they would like to try some new lifetime guarantee socks or comfortable padded inserts; a shirt sales rep shows a customer a matching tie; an auto mechanic recommends an extended warranty, etc.

Sometimes our add-on sales opportunities aren't quite so obvious. Be creative. To get you thinking along these lines, make a list of possible add-on sales for your products. As with any creative effort, the first few ideas will come easily, but push yourself to expand the list as far as possible. If you come up with 10 ideas, try for 20. Often it's the last few ideas, painfully pulled out, that work the best.

47. Stay close after the sale

Customers hate a love-'em-and-leave-'em relationship, yet most salespeople offer just that. Once the sale is made the customer goes back to feeling like a stranger. Look for opportunities to contact the customer after the sale. Establish an ongoing friendship and they'll keep coming back.

Some ideas for contacting customers after the sale:

• Mail thank-you notes.
• Call to be sure the product/service met their needs.
• Send out new-product information.
• Send clippings of interest or newsworthy information that may reassure customers of their good purchasing decision.
• Send birthday and holiday cards.
• Invite them to participate in focus groups.
• Call to thank them for referrals.

48. Ask for referrals

Always ask satisfied customers for names of people who might also like to buy from you. Get addresses and phone numbers and follow through with a call or a card.

While this is a common practice among large ticket sales, it can also be used in hundreds of other situations. Suppose you call people to introduce yourself and invite them to come to your business. Most people will be surprised and pleased by a personal invitation like that. And it beats sitting around hoping someone will come in.

Of course, the more information you can get about a referred person the better. But don't make referral-giving a big job for your customer. A name and address or phone number is all you need. You can look up other data if necessary.

49. Maintain a positive attitude about selling as a career

Many people avoid selling because of some imagined negative stereotype about salespeople. Customer contact people refuse to call themselves salespeople. Yet everyone is in sales to some degree. We constantly sell other people on ourselves and our companies.

Like any profession, selling requires professional skills and attitudes. But often these skills and attitudes are different than one might think. For example, it surprises some people to find that you do not need to be an extrovert to be successful at selling. Quiet, thoughtful people often are very successful. A quiet self-confidence is more important than "techniques."

You will likely be good at sales if you agree with statements like these:[11]

- I can convert strangers into friends quickly and easily.

- I can attract and hold the attention of others even when I have not met them.

- I love new situations.

- I'm intrigued with the psychology of meeting and building a good relationship with someone I do not know.

- I would enjoy making a sales presentation to a group of executives.

---

[11] These ideas were found in Elwood N. Chapman, *The Fifty Minute Sales Training Program*, published by Crisp Publications, Inc.

- When dressed for the occasion, I have great confidence in myself.
- I do not mind using the telephone to make appointments with people I don't know.
- I enjoy solving problems.
- Most of the time, I feel secure.

There is certainly nothing demeaning about selling a product or service. There is no shame in telling your friends that you are in sales. If you harbor such feelings, it's time for an attitude check.

Selling is an honorable profession that helps people solve problems and make decisions that will benefit them. The best sellers are helpers, just as the best customer service people are.

Section V

The 50 Powerful Ideas Summarized

50. Do unto others

The Bible teaches the most succinct of all the *50 Powerful Ideas:*

"Therefore all things whatsoever ye would have that men should do to you, do ye even so to them."

—Matthew 7:12

Thus, the skills for creating customer satisfaction are the master.keys to all career success.

I hope you'll reread these *50 Powerful Ideas* and use them starting today. You'll experience greater fulfillment and success in all that you do.

But that's just part of the challenge. Getting your entire team (department, company, agency, organization) to *use* these and related ideas is ultimately the key to organizational success. In the bonus chapter on the following pages, I will show you a step-by-step process for creating a customer culture in your organization.

Translate Good Intentions Into a Customer Strategy That Works!

The bank executives felt the new slogan the ad agency had come up with would be a good one. But when a customer asked a teller "What's this 'we give 110 percent service' mean?" the teller looked dumbfounded. "I don't know," she replied. "I just saw the billboard on the way to work this morning myself."

Top management at a large retailer put out a clear edict: All clerks are to say "Thank you for shopping at _____" to every customer. That's an order. Unfortunately, the minimum-wage clerks often uttered the mandatory phrase mechanically and without feeling.

The most powerful way to prosper in a slow growth economy is to enhance customer satisfaction and retention. But making a commitment to better customer service involves much more than mouthing a motto, slogan or mechanical phrase. The real management challenge lies in translating the slogans into actions that create customer satisfaction and loyalty—in creating a strategy for implementing good service intentions.

This chapter shows a logical, theoretically sound approach to building and implementing what I call an *E-Plus Customer Satisfaction* strategy. Any organization can do it and the payoff is enormous.

To implement an *E-Plus* strategy, follow these steps:

1. *Introduce your employees to the E-Plus concept.* Training and reading materials can get everyone in the organization speaking the same language—singing from the same sheet music. Start by having each person in your organization read this book carefully. Since many people do not digest written material very well, you may want to supplement the book with the

videotape training program. The basic ideas in this book set a foundation for ongoing growth in customer service.

Build your customer efforts around the *E-Plus* concept. Be sure everyone understands the basics of *E-Plus*.

2. *Focus initially on six areas where little things can make a difference:* VISPAC. Working with clients, I have identified six areas where *E-Plus* opportunities can be found. To help remember these I use the acronym VISPAC (as in creating a visible package). Below are some examples of VISPAC expectations exceeded.

- **Value**. When I ask people to describe value that exceeds their expectations, I hear tales of exceptional products like 15-year-old Kirby vacuum cleaners and 20-year-old Western Auto freezers. Often people talk about their Ford or Toyota pickup truck with 200,000 miles on it or a sweater that dates back a quarter century. Each of these products exceeded their customer's expectations of value. They got more than they expected for their money. How can your business give more value than expected?

- **Information**. My son recently had knee surgery. The therapist not only explained what exercises he should do but also gave him photocopied sheets illustrating exactly how do them. She wrote his name at the top of each sheet and numbered the sequence. Enlightened auto salespeople spend time with their customers—after the sale—explaining all the features on the new car. A hospital client changed the signs and installed color stripes on the corridor floors to direct people to various departments. A cellular phone dealer calls customers to see if they understand how to use their phone's features and offers to meet to explain them in person. How can your business give customers more useful information?

- **Speed**. A well-known air freight company claims to deliver packages by 10 a.m. the next morning, but often arrives by 9 or 9:30. The repair office for a major office equipment company makes it a point to have the service person arrive earlier than promised. At a supermarket, additional cashiers open when more than two customers are in line. Fast-food restaurants have your lunch up almost before you can order it. Are there ways you can give customers a little faster service than they expect?

- **Price**. Auto dealers faced with sticker-shocked customers have learned to express prices in terms of monthly payments or lease rates, not the full price. A repair shop tells customers the job will cost "about $50" and then comes in at $47.50. Customers are astonished. It actually cost *less* than expected! (Note if the price comes in at $50.50, you've lost the *E-Plus*. The amount isn't as important as the fact that it went over estimate.) How can your organization exceed pricing expectations?

- **Add-ons**. Sometimes add-ons are sold, sometimes given away. A shoe store clerk gives a shoehorn. A clerk at a supermarket hands the customer a few candy kisses with the receipt—an unexpected thank-you. The paint store clerk checks to be sure the customer has caulking and sandpaper, which might have been forgotten. What add-on products or services can you give your customers?

- **Convenience.** The typical response to a customer with a faulty product is "bring it in and we'll replace it." That is "E" but not *E-Plus*. Toyota's Lexus division did it better when handling a recall shortly after coming onto the market with their new car. Dealers called customers for appointments to pick up their cars. They left a loaner car, and some dealers even left a rose or a $50 bill on the seat to apologize for the inconvenience! The outcome: Customers were exposed to the exceptional service department and an embarrassment became what one Toyota executive called "a watershed event" for getting customers into the dealer's shop. How can you make things more convenient for your customers?

Be sure your people understand *E-Plus* and VISPAC. Generate discussion about these ideas. Get people speaking the same language.

3. Add management attention, encouragement and a reward system that reinforces participation in idea sharing. Hold regular *E-Plus* brainstorming sessions. Be receptive and imaginative to employee ideas.

Remember to reward the right behaviors as we discussed in Idea #26. Rewards don't always need to be monetary—often compliments and recognition are even more appreciated.

4. *Celebrate with hoopla.* Make customer appreciation efforts fun and recognize peoples' participation and successes. One of my clients built its culture around the term Excel. The Excel philosophy included ongoing recognition where people received "points" for such things as:

- Compliments received from customers (written or spoken).
- Participation in idea-sharing meetings.
- Participation in explorer groups.
- Contributing stories to the company newsletter.
- Being selected as "employee of the month" (or week or quarter) by their managers.
- Submitting written suggestions.
- Attending optional training.
- Bringing in new customers.
- Reading information bulletins, etc.

At the end of each month, managers tallied the points and nominated one employee from each department to attend the "Excelebration." This celebration was held during a lunch hour and included a free buffet and games for prizes. They had turkey shoots, fish ponds and roulette wheels that gave participants chances to win cash and gifts.

At the end of the fiscal year, a big "Excelebration" was held for people who had won the monthly contests most frequently. The prizes given included televisions, bicycles, exercise equipment, airline tickets, vacation packages, etc.

Note: This was not a huge corporation and the budget was not unlimited, but the money spent was well worth the effort and the program continues. Employees talked about these sessions for weeks.

5. *Constantly sharpen your picture of what customers expect and how you are doing.* Use naive listening, open-ended questions, focus groups and exploration groups to monitor customers and competitor ideas.

Ideally you can get some feedback from almost every customer. But don't rely on feedback cards like those found in many restaurants and hotels. These tend to be completed mostly by people who are either very pleased or very upset. The data can distort the reality.

A better approach was used by a car dealership's service department. The shop did some research and found that three major things most accurately determined customer satisfaction: The work was done on time, the price was fair and the car owner's inconvenience was minimized. Each customer was asked to complete a brief, three-item questionnaire at the time they paid for their service. The form had a place for their suggestions, if any.

Virtually all customers complied and the short form focused only on the key indicators. The card, of course, was changed periodically to gather data about other concerns.

So look for the most important determinants of satisfaction. Then monitor how you are doing.

6. *Hire people who have good attitudes toward customers.* If possible, hire people who you've seen dealing with customers—and reward them for their efforts. Keep a card file or list of people who have given you particularly good service. Consider hiring from less frequently used groups. Often people with disabilities and "seasoned" citizens have excellent customer skills. Don't get too hung up on particular levels of formal education. I once hired an accountant who had not finished his college degree over several applicants who had impressive school credentials. The result: This man was aware of his lower level of education and made up for it by really going the extra mile in serving the company.

A great attitude—especially one of gratitude for customers—is the single most important ingredient in exceptional public contact employees.

7. *Make customer satisfaction an ongoing priority, not just a "program."*
Try to avoid using the word "program." Instead think of your ongoing efforts as the evolution of a constantly improving customer culture. Think long-term, not just to next month's or next year's profits.

I am reminded of the chairman of a huge Japanese manufacturing company who was asked if he had long-range goals, He replied, "Yes." "How long?" he was asked. "Two-hundred fifty years," he replied. The astonished reporter asked, "What will it take to achieve these?" "Patience," he said.

Think long-term; think ongoing growth; think *E-Plus*. *E-Plus* thinking forms the basis for a strategy, not just a slogan. If you're not thinking *E-Plus*, your competition may be.

Translating slogans into strategy

An *E-Plus* strategy invites all employees to consistently ask two crucial questions: "What does my customer expect?" and, "How can I exceed those expectations?"

Exceeding in small ways is sufficient. The little things mean a great deal to customers. I hope this small book will trigger some big thinking. Test these ideas and let me know how things work out.

Consumer survey

Major turnoffs in customer service

The following is part of an ongoing research project focusing on what most turns you off as a customer. If you would like to be a part of this study, photocopy this questionnaire and send it to me.

Following are examples of eight types of businesses you have dealt with as a customer. Please rank the top three things that are most likely to cause you *dissatisfaction* as you deal with each type of organization described. Use the following list:

F = **F**riendliness/lack of courtesy/attention
H = Un**H**elpful employees /lack knowledge
M = **M**annerisms/employee appearance
P = **P**rice too high for value received
G = Bad **G**uarantee/failure to back up products
Q = **Q**uality not as good as expected
S = **S**low service/help not available
D = **D**irty business place, messy/cluttered
A = Poor **A**vailability of product/small selection
L = **L**ocation inconvenient, layout, parking, access

For example, if your greatest turnoff was "quality not as good as you expected," your second greatest turnoff was "price too high for value received," and your third greatest turnoff was "slow service," you would respond:

Turnoff #1: Q_ Turnoff #2: P_Turnoff #3: S_

1. **Self-service retail.** Examples: supermarkets (Albertson's, Publix), discount stores (K-Mart, Wal-Mart), warehouse stores (Pace, Sam's, Costco).

   Turnoff #1: ___ Turnoff #2: ___ Turnoff #3: ___

2. **Fast-food restaurants.** Examples: Wendy's, Arby's, TCBY yogurt shops, take-out pizza stores, cafeterias.

   Turnoff #1: ___ Turnoff #2: ___ Turnoff #3: ___

3. **Full-service retail.** Examples: full-line department stores (Nordstrom, Macy's, Nieman-Marcus), retailers that provide individualized service (florists, jewelers).

   Turnoff #1: ___ Turnoff #2: ___ Turnoff #3: ___

4. **Public services.** Examples: offices of public utilities (gas company, electric company), some government agencies (state license bureau, employment services).

   Turnoff #1: ___ Turnoff #2: ___ Turnoff #3: ___

5. **Full-service restaurants.** Examples: eat-in restaurants with servers (Red Lobster, hotel dining rooms).

   Turnoff #1: ___ Turnoff #2: ___ Turnoff #3: ___

6.   **Repair services**. Examples: auto repair shops, business machines repair organizations.

Turnoff #1: ___ Turnoff #2: ___ Turnoff #3: ___

7.   **Financial institutions**. Examples: banks, savings and loans, credit unions, insurance agencies.

Turnoff #1: ___ Turnoff #2: ___ Turnoff #3: ___

8.   **Personal services and health care**. Examples: hospitals, beauty shops, opticians, dentists.

Turnoff #1: ___ Turnoff #2: ___ Turnoff #3: ___

How to translate good intentions into a customer strategy

Please complete the following. I am:

_____ Male   _____ Female

_____ Under age 20   _____ Between 20-35

_____ Between 36-50   _____ Over 50 years

Education attained (years):

_____High school or less   _____Some college

_____College graduate   _____Advanced degree

Household income:

_____Less than $20,000/yr   _____$20,000 to $40,000/yr

_____$40,001 to $60,000/yr   _____More than $60,000/yr

As a general statement, how would you describe the quality of customer service you experience?

Very Poor   1 2 3 4 5 6 7   Very Good

Please name the customer service turnoff you find most irritating: (this may be different from those listed in this questionnaire):_____

_____

_____

Mail to:
   Dr. Paul R. Timm
   81 E. 2000 South
   Orem, UT 84058

or Fax to:
   (801) 378-8309

Thank you!

About the author

DR. PAUL R. TIMM has written 24 books and scores of articles on customer service, human relations, communication and self-management. He holds a doctorate degree from Florida State University in organizational communication and is currently chairman of the Department of Management Communication in the Marriott School of Management at Brigham Young University.

As an active consultant and trainer, Timm has worked with thousands of people from organizations throughout North America. He wrote and appears in six videotape programs sold worldwide including: *The Power of Customer Service, Successful Self-Management* and the tape program based on this book, *50 Ways to Keep Your Customers (and Get New Ones)*, produced by JWA Video of Chicago (call 312-829-5100 for information). Timm also authored the popular Career Press books, *51 Ways to Save Your Job* and *50 Ways to Win New Customers*.

Dr. Timm and Customer SatisfACTION Strategies, Inc., are happy to help you with customer service training and consulting. For further information or to arrange an organizational assessment, contact Dr. Timm at:

81 East 2000 South
Orem, UT 84058
801-378-5682 or 226-0819
Fax: (801) 378-8309

Also, please send any comments about this book to the above address. We really want to know how you like our product and how we could serve you better.

117

Index

touch, 48
unreasonable, 75-76

D

Diversity, 42-43

E

E-Plus, 22, 27, 30, 54-55,
61-62, 104-107, 111
Equity Theory, 28-30
Expectations, 109-110
Explorer groups, 88
External customers. 10-11
Eye contact, 33-34

F

Feedback, 51-52
Focus groups, 89-92
Following through, 52-53,
61

G

Greetings, 32-34

H

Hiring, 110-111
Hoopla, 87-88, 108

I

In Search of Excellence, 87
Internal customers, 10-11
Involvement, 37

L

Listening, 45-46
Long-term, 110-111
Lost customers, 15-22

M

Management, 63-94
breaks, 76
caring culture, 79-80
correspondence, 92-93
enriching people's
jobs, 80-81
explorer groups, 88
focus groups, 89-92
hiring, 110
hoopla and fun, 87-88,
108
long view, 81
long-term goals, 110-111
recognition, 82-88
recruitment, 77
reinforcement, 82-88
rewards, 68-70, 82-88,
108-109
themes, 64-68
taboos, 74-75
tools, 76-77
training, 70-74
user groups, 89

N

Names, 45, 93

NOW YOU CAN VIEW
"50 WAYS TO KEEP YOUR CUSTOMERS"
by Dr. Paul R. Timm
ON VIDEOCASSETTE

Rated in 1994 by <u>Training Media Review</u> of Boston as one of "the best videos of 1993," **50 Ways to Keep Your Customers** with Dr. Paul R. Timm provides the common sense information to help anyone improve their customer service.

Numbered one to fifty, each skill in this 60-minute program can be put to use immediately. They are practical, workable techniques that take the mystery out of how to give exceptional service.

The **50 Ways to Keep Your Customers** video training program with Dr. Paul R. Timm (comes complete with video, audio and additional copy of his book) has been designed to be used by both individuals for self-instruction and trainers for training sessions. This video is loaded with graphics and realistic vignettes to make learning easy, fun and memorable.

To Order: Call Toll-Free 1-800-327-5110 or FAX Your Order to 1-312-829-9074

Yes, send me _____ **50 Ways to Keep Your Customers** video training programs at $99.95 each.

Name _____

Company _____

Address _____

City _____ State _____ Zip _____

Day Phone _____

___ Enclosed Check   PO Number _____

___ Please charge my credit card   VISA ___ Mastercard ____

Card Number _____ Exp Date _____

Or send to: JWA Video, 411 S. Sangamon St, #2B, Chicago, IL 60607

CP